MEXICAN IMMIGRANTS
IN THEIR SHOES

BY CYNTHIA KENNEDY HENZEL

Published by The Child's World®
1980 Lookout Drive • Mankato, MN 56003-1705
800-599-READ • www.childsworld.com

Content Consultant: Dr. Anne M. Martínez, Professor of American Political Culture and
Theory, University of Groningen

Photographs ©: Peter M. Fredin/AP Images, cover, 1; AP Images, 6, 8, 11, 16; Horst
Faas/AP Images, 12; B. M. Design/iStockphoto, 15; Rich Pedroncelli/AP Images, 18;
James Steidl/Shutterstock Images, 21; Red Line Editorial, 22; iStockphoto, 24; Evan
Vucci/AP Images, 27; Claudia Torrens/AP Images, 28

ISBN 9781503820302
LCCN 2016960930

Printed in the United States of America
PA02338

ABOUT THE AUTHOR

Cynthia Kennedy Henzel has a bachelor of science degree in social studies
education and a master of science degree in geography. She has worked as
a teacher-educator in many countries. Currently, she works writing books and
developing education materials for social studies, science, and ELL students.
She has written more than 80 books for young people.

TABLE OF CONTENTS

FAST FACTS

Reasons for Immigrating

- The Bracero Program (1942–1964) brought millions of Mexican immigrants to the United States. Most worked in agriculture.

- After 1965, immigration increased as U.S. citizens **sponsored** family members in Mexico.

- U.S. companies still had a high demand for immigrant labor after the Bracero Program ended. Many immigrants came illegally.

Where Mexican Immigrants Settled

- Many immigrants live in states that were once part of Mexico, such as California and Texas.

- Florida, New York, and Illinois also have large populations of Mexican immigrants.

Important Numbers

- In 2014, approximately 52 percent of **undocumented** immigrants in the United States were from Mexico.

- Mexican immigration has decreased since 2009. More Mexicans have migrated from the United States to Mexico than from Mexico to the United States.

TIMELINE

1848: The Mexican–American War ends. Mexico loses territory that later becomes part of seven U.S. states.

1853–1854: The United States purchases land from Mexico. This land becomes part of Arizona and New Mexico.

1942: The Bracero Program begins.

1962: Cesar Chavez begins a labor **union** that is later known as United Farm Workers.

1964: The Bracero Program ends.

1965: The Immigration and Nationality Act ends immigration laws based on race or ethnicity.

2001: The Dream Act is introduced in the U.S. Congress but does not pass.

2007: The number of Mexican immigrants begins declining.

2012: President Barack Obama begins Deferred Action for Childhood Arrivals (DACA).

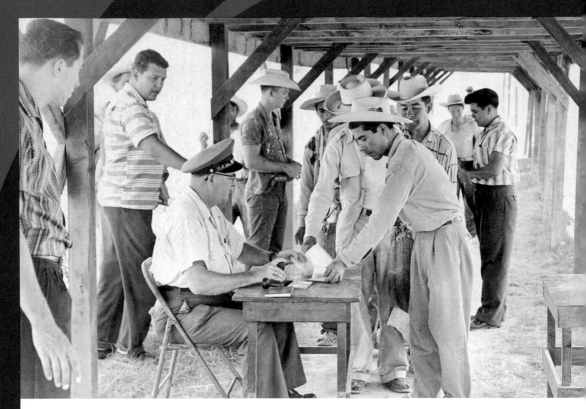

Chapter 1

THE BRACERO

R igoberto Garcia Perez stood in the dusty yard. He watched as his father disappeared down the rutted road. His father was heading to the United States to work as a bracero. The U.S. government had first introduced the Bracero Program in 1942. The program allowed Mexican men to work on farms in the United States.

Rigoberto hoped his father would return soon. His father wanted to earn enough money to buy back the farmland he had lost during the 1930s. Rigoberto wondered how long that would take.

His father returned to Mexico a year and a half later. He had not earned enough money to buy back the land, but he started a small store in Mexico with his earnings. Rigoberto's father believed that working for himself was the best way to get ahead. "When you work for someone else, the profit from your work stays with them," he said.[1]

But Rigoberto was curious about working in the United States. So, when he grew up, he caught a train to the Mexico–United States border. In the 1950s, the border was not well guarded, so he simply walked across. Rigoberto hopped trains and traveled to northern California. There he found a job picking cherries. It was hard work, but he earned more than he would have in Mexico.

Rigoberto later returned to Mexico and got married. However, Mexico was a poor country with few jobs. He decided to work in the United States as a bracero. Rigoberto climbed on a bus with other braceros and headed for California.

When they arrived, the man in charge told them to take off their clothes. Another man sprayed them with smelly chemicals to kill lice. A third person stuck a needle in his arm and drew blood to test for diseases.

The farm bosses arrived, and the braceros lined up. The bosses rejected men who looked old or weak. A strawberry grower chose Rigoberto, and Rigoberto signed a contract to work 45 days for 80 cents an hour.

At the farm's bunkhouse, beds lined the walls from floor to ceiling. The boss pointed out Rigoberto's bed. Rigoberto crawled beneath the thin blanket and slept.

A loud horn woke him early in the morning. He ate breakfast and went to the field. By noon, his back ached from stooping to pick the strawberries. The bosses were always watching, so he worked fast. At noon, he ate his lunch quickly and then went back to work. A typical workday lasted from sunrise until dark.

One man complained about working 14 hours per day with few breaks. The bosses wanted the workers to do what they were told with no complaining. They sent the man back to Mexico. "There was always **exploitation** then," said Rigoberto.[2] One night, many of the braceros became sick from spoiled food.

◄ **A bracero harvests crops on a farm in southern California.**

9

One person even died. Rigoberto was scared, thinking of dying so far away from his family.

When Rigoberto returned to Mexico, he and his wife planted crops on rented land. But crop prices were unpredictable. One year, they planted sweet potatoes and made some money. Another year, they planted onions but lost money. Rigoberto returned to the United States to find work. "I went as a bracero four times, but I didn't like it," he said.[3]

One farmer felt sorry for the hard work and low wages of the braceros. In 1959, he helped Rigoberto get documents to stay in the United States permanently. Rigoberto wanted to bring his wife to the United States. "I was tired of being alone," he said.[4]

Rigoberto's wife soon joined him. His five children stayed with a relative until they could get papers to join the family. But in time, the children joined their parents in the United States. Eventually, the family bought a house. The youngest child, who had been seven years old when she arrived, went on to graduate from college. "It was important to send my kids to school," Rigoberto said. "That's what I was trying to do as a bracero. I wanted a real future."[5]

Braceros often had to work bent over for many hours a day to ▶ earn money for their families.

Chapter 2

FARM WORKERS UNITE

Agustín Ramírez said good-bye to his parents, brothers, and sisters. He was upset that his parents were making him return to Mexico alone. He didn't want to go. The year was 1969, and Agustín was 13 years old. The Vietnam War (1954–1975) was raging, and Agustín's parents feared he would eventually have to fight in the war if he stayed in the United States.

◄ Fear of being forced to fight in the Vietnam War led many people, including immigrants, to leave the United States.

Agustín had been born in Mexico. But since 1963, his whole family had lived in the United States. For a year, they lived in a farm camp. Agustín and his siblings helped pick figs and peaches. His father soon had enough money to buy the family its first car. Agustín loved driving through the fields with his family, scaring the rabbits with the bright lights.

In 1964, the family had moved into their own house. Agustín started school that year. He made friends, and he did well academically. It wasn't long before Agustín spoke English better than his parents did. He even **interpreted** for them when they bought their house. Agustín was happy with his life in the United States.

Unfortunately, his parents had different ideas.

"Papi said we had broken the law by coming to the United States, but back then I didn't understand much about laws. All I could think of was why there would be a law that would prevent children from being with their father."

—Reyna Grande, who was brought to United States by her father when she was a child[6]

13

They had always planned to return to Mexico once they made money in the United States. Sending Agustín back to Mexico was the first step. They wanted him to finish school in Mexico and then go to college. They believed they could live a better life in Mexico than they could in the United States.

Agustín went back to Mexico and lived with one of his mother's friends. In the United States, he had been very poor. "Yet in Mexico," he said, "I had the ability to go to the most expensive school in my town, where all the rich kids were."[7] By 1972, a sister and a brother had joined him. His parents and four other siblings were still in the United States.

Agustín finished college with a degree in agronomy, the study of farming. After college, he thought about working for the Mexican government. He knew government jobs would pay well and allow him to live a good life. Unfortunately, the Mexican government had no jobs to offer. Agustín returned to the United States.

In the United States, Agustín needed two more years of study to use his college degree. But it was too expensive to go back to college. His parents had sacrificed for 12 years to support his education in Mexico. But now he was back picking grapes beside his father in Napa Valley, California. It was a hard blow. Agustín felt he had disappointed his parents.

▲ **Napa Valley, located in northern California, is famous for producing grapes.**

In Napa Valley, there was a union known as the United Farm Workers. This union had organized the workers to demand more money. Agustín's father and uncles had long supported unions. They had gone on **strike** to fight for better wages. The union leaders asked Agustín to work on a new contract. He helped negotiate the contract in English. Then he explained the contract to the workers in Spanish. Agustín also participated in a march.

This march was held to celebrate the new contract. One of the marchers was Cesar Chavez, the man who started the United Farm Workers. Agustín was excited when Chavez asked him to work for him.

Agustín liked the work. He felt like he was giving back to his people after the sacrifices his parents had made. But being a union organizer did not pay well, and he now had a wife and children. He and his wife thought of returning to Mexico to find better jobs. They could live in a bigger house and have more comfortable lives.

Over time, though, they decided to stay in the United States. Their family was there. It was home. "When you transplant a plant, and you treat it right, it's going to grow roots," Agustín explained. "That's what happened to us. We were transplanted. Our roots are over there, but the tree that grew up is over here. And my kids' roots are here now."[8]

◄ **Cesar Chavez spent many years fighting for better rights for farm workers.**

Chapter 3

FAMILY TIES

Raquel Rodríguez squirmed to find a comfortable place to sleep. She was lying on the old mattress that she shared with her mother and eight younger siblings. The sound of raindrops pounded on the tin roof of their one-room house in Monterrey, Mexico. Raquel moved an empty coffee can to catch the drips that came through the ceiling.

◀ **Many immigrants begin their lives in the United States by working low-paying jobs at restaurants.**

The year was 1974, and Raquel was 14 years old. As she lay awake, she realized she would have to quit school and go to work. If she didn't, her family would lose even this poor shelter.

Raquel found a job as a cook, but she struggled to make enough to keep their house. However, her luck began to change in her early 20s. She got married and had a baby daughter. Her husband had a sister who was a U.S. citizen. The sister sponsored Raquel, her husband, and their daughter to immigrate to the United States. The family moved to Texas to start a new life.

Raquel and her family arrived in the United States with nothing. They slept on the floor of her husband's parents' one-bedroom apartment. Raquel's husband found a job working on cars, and Raquel worked as a waitress. Their life improved, but Raquel could not forget her family still living in poverty in Mexico. "I had nothing once," she said. "Now I can't bear to see them have nothing."[9]

Raquel was a **permanent resident** of the United States, but she was not a U.S. citizen. She knew she would have to live five years in the United States and take tests to become a citizen. And only citizens can sponsor other family members to immigrate.

Raquel encouraged her family to come anyway, even though they could not come legally. She thought any work in the United States was better than living in poverty in Mexico. Raquel's brother came first with his wife and child. They slept on a mattress on the floor, next to Raquel and her family.

Raquel and her husband eventually moved into an apartment of their own. However, they didn't have a lot of extra space. Even so, Raquel's sister Irma sent her daughter to live with them so she could go to school. Soon, Irma came with two more daughters. Then Raquel's sister Veronica came with her husband and three children.

Veronica's husband found a good job. Her children did well in school. The family saved money, paid taxes, worked hard, and bought a house. Even so, they felt like they had to live in the shadows. They were always fearful that something would happen to send them back to poverty in Mexico. Even a traffic stop might bring them to the attention of authorities. "My husband just called to tell me he saw (officers)," Veronica said.[10]

Raquel felt guilty that she could move about freely but her sisters' families could not. She could find a job with benefits and health care, but Veronica struggled to pay for her son's hospital bill after he needed surgery. Still, Raquel knew Veronica felt lucky.

▲ Mexicans wait to pass through inspection and cross the border from Tijuana, Mexico, into the United States.

"Living here without papers is still better than living (in Mexico)," Veronica said.[11]

Raquel's sister Irma worked two jobs to support her daughters. She learned to drive, bought two cars, and rented her own small house. Then her two older daughters, who were both in high school, decided to get married and move out.

TOTAL POPULATION OF MEXICAN IMMIGRANTS IN THE UNITED STATES

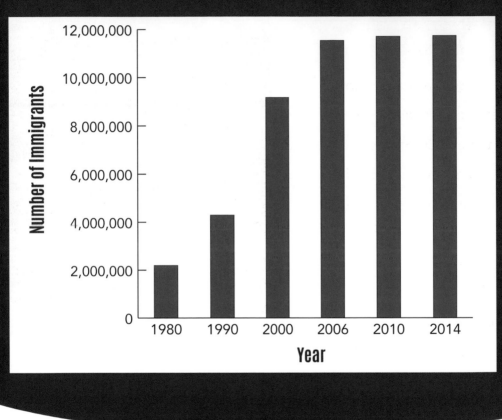

"I was so depressed," said Irma, "All I wanted was to pick up my stuff and leave."[12] Irma gave up. After living in the United States for six years, she went back to Mexico. It was not long before she dreamed of returning to the United States with her youngest daughter.

But returning meant she would have to do so illegally. She would need to get fake papers and hire someone to take her family across the border. That was expensive. She hoped Raquel would become a citizen and sponsor her family to immigrate.

Raquel remained torn between her good life in the United States and her family responsibilities. She sent money and gifts to family in Mexico and bought a house in Mexico for her mother. She felt at home in Mexico and often celebrated holidays there.

"The main reason for my return is family. I could help them while I was (in the United States), but family comes before money."

—José Arellano Correa, who returned to Mexico in 2005[14]

Although her heart remained in Mexico, she knew she must stay in the United States for her family to survive. She was the root of the family, the one they all depended on. "My family is always first," she said. "Always."[13]

Chapter 4

DREAMERS

In 2005, 11-year-old Antonio Alarcón followed his parents through the Mexican desert. "I remember that one warm evening when we started walking across the border," Antonio said. "The silence of the desert warned us of the danger we faced, and we knew we had to be very careful."[15] He listened for rattlesnakes or robbers. Antonio's parents told him to stay close.

Antonio was scared. He missed his grandparents, who had raised him since he was a baby. He also missed his little brother, who was not old enough for the dangerous desert crossing. Antonio had one bottle of water and a few cans of food. After three days of walking, they were out of supplies. Still, they walked another half a day. Their only water came from a muddy canal.

Finally, they were in Arizona. Then they crammed into a car with six other people. They were lucky. Many immigrants had to walk across the Arizona desert where temperatures often topped 120 degrees Fahrenheit (49°C). Hundreds died.

After Antonio's family arrived in California, they traveled by airplane to New York City. The giant buildings were a shock for Antonio. But he loved it. His mother worked in a laundromat 12 hours a day, six days a week. His father worked in construction. Many bosses hired undocumented workers because they worked for less money. Antonio's father was often cheated out of his wages. But he was afraid to complain because he feared being reported to immigration officials. He was even afraid to go to the doctor when he hurt his ankle.

Antonio and his parents missed their family in Mexico. When his grandfather died, it was awful not being able to say goodbye.

> "I'm an American, and I don't need a piece of paper or a judge's approval to confirm it. I am because that's what's in my heart! This is my country!"
>
> —Joel Cruz, a Dreamer from California[17]

"The most painful thing was seeing my father collapse and cry," said Antonio.[16] But without immigration papers, the family knew it would be too difficult to return to the United States.

Then the next year, Antonio's grandmother died. Antonio's parents faced an awful choice. They wanted Antonio to finish his education in the United States. But there was no one to care for their younger son in Mexico. Antonio's parents decided to return to Mexico, leaving 18-year-old Antonio behind.

Antonio moved in with his uncles. He finished high school, but his parents did not see him graduate. He missed them terribly, but he knew that he had more opportunities for education and work in the United States. In Mexico, his father now worked on a farm and his mother ran a small store. They had enough to survive but would never get ahead.

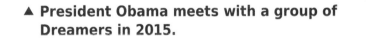

▲ **President Obama meets with a group of Dreamers in 2015.**

Antonio received the offer of a **scholarship** for a two-year college, but he could not get it without immigration papers. Then, in 2012, U.S. President Barack Obama began a policy known as the Deferred Action for Childhood Arrivals (DACA). DACA was meant to help people known as Dreamers. These were people who had entered the United States before they were 16 years old. DACA would allow Dreamers to work or go to school without fear of **deportation** for at least two years.

▲ After Donald Trump won the 2016 presidential election, many Dreamers feared they would not be allowed back into the United States if they traveled abroad.

Antonio started college. Two years later, he visited his parents and brother in Mexico at Christmas. He gave his mother a special gift: his college diploma. Then he returned to New York to continue his education at a four-year college. Antonio joined other Dreamers pushing for changes to immigration laws so that he could become a U.S. citizen and reunite with his family.

Approximately 5.6 million Mexican immigrants in the United States are undocumented. As of 2016, DACA had allowed 569,000 young people like Antonio to stay.

Immigration from Mexico has decreased in recent years. Part of the reason is that there are fewer job opportunities in the United States. Another reason is that there has been more immigration enforcement on the border. Even so, more than 11.7 million Mexican immigrants lived in the United States as of 2014. This made Mexican Americans the largest immigrant group in the country.

THINK ABOUT IT

- Why do you think many immigrants were willing to leave part of their family in Mexico when they moved to the United States? What would you have done if you were in their situation?
- Do you think the Bracero Program was a success or a failure? Why?
- If people are brought to the United States as children, what hardships might they face if they are deported?

GLOSSARY

deportation (dee-por-TAY-shun): Deportation is when a person is forced to leave a country. The immigrant faced deportation back to Mexico because he was in the United States illegally.

exploitation (ex-ploy-TAY-shun): Exploitation is the act of using someone's services unfairly. Immigrants suffered exploitation because they were afraid to complain.

interpreted (in-TER-pruh-tid): Interpreted means explaining another language to help someone understand. Agustín interpreted for his parents because they did not speak English well.

permanent resident (PUR-muh-nent REZ-uh-dent): A permanent resident is an immigrant who is allowed to live and work in the United States permanently. Raquel had to be a permanent resident before she could become a citizen.

scholarship (SKAHL-er-ship): A scholarship is money given by an organization to help a student pay for school. Antonio received a scholarship, so he did not have to pay the full cost of his education.

sponsored (SPON-surd): Sponsored means took responsibility for someone so they could immigrate legally. Raquel was able to immigrate to the United States because her sister sponsored her.

strike (STRYK): A strike is when workers refuse to work in the hope that employers will meet their demands. The workers went on strike and demanded more money.

undocumented (un-DOK-yoo-men-ted): Undocumented means without legal permission to live or work in the United States. Many undocumented workers are afraid they will be deported.

union (YOON-yun): A union is an organization formed to protect workers' rights. The union pushed for higher wages for its members.

SOURCE NOTES

1. Rigoberto Garcia Perez. "Immigrants: The Story of a Bracero." *David Bacon*. David Bacon, 18 Apr. 2001. Web. 19 Jan. 2017.

2. Ibid.

3. Ibid.

4. Ibid.

5. Ibid.

6. Reyna Grande. *The Distance Between Us*. New York, NY: Washington Square Press, 2012. Print. 165–166.

7. "Interview with Agustín Ramírez." *David Bacon*. David Bacon, 21 Nov. 2001. Web. 19 Jan. 2017.

8. Ibid.

9. Julia Preston. "Making a Life in the U.S., but Feeling Mexico's Tug." *New York Times*. New York Times Company, 19 Dec. 2006. Web. 19 Jan. 2017.

10. Lizette Alvarez. "Fear and Hope in Immigrant's Furtive Existence." *New York Times*. New York Times Company, 20 Dec. 2006. Web. 19 Jan. 2017.

11. Ibid.

12. Mireya Navarro. "For Divided Family, Border Is Sorrowful Barrier." *New York Times*. New York Times Company, 21 Dec. 2006. Web. 19 Jan. 2017.

13. Julia Preston. "Making a Life in the U.S., but Feeling Mexico's Tug." *New York Times*. New York Times Company, 19 Dec. 2006. Web. 19 Jan. 2017.

14. "More Mexicans Leaving U.S. Than Entering, Study Says." *FOX News*. FOX News Network, 20 Nov. 2015. Web. 19 Jan. 2017.

15. Antonio Alarcón. "My Immigration Story." *Make the Road*. Make the Road, 2 Apr. 2014. Web. 19 Jan. 2017.

16. Ibid.

17. Sam Schlinkert. "Letters from DREAMers: Young Immigrants Hope for Deferred Action." *Daily Beast*. Daily Beast Company, 17 Aug. 2012. Web. 19 Jan. 2017.

TO LEARN MORE

Books

Metz, Lorijo. *A Nation of Immigrants*. New York, NY: PowerKids Press, 2014.

Robinson, Joanna J. *Mexico*. Mankato, MN: The Child's World, 2016.

Roza, Greg. *Immigration and Migration*. New York, NY: Gareth Stevens Publishing, 2011.

Web Sites

Visit our Web site for links about Mexican immigrants:
childsworld.com/links

Note to Parents, Teachers, and Librarians: We routinely verify our Web links to make sure they are safe and active sites. So encourage your readers to check them out!

INDEX